RELEASED FROM CIRCULATION

THE ELECTROMAGNETIC SPECTRUM

UNDERSTANDING AND USING MICROWAVES

ALISON AND STEPHEN ELDRIDGE

Published in 2022 by Enslow Publishing, LLC.
101 W. 23rd Street, Suite 240, New York, NY 10011

Copyright © 2022 by Enslow Publishing, LLC

All rights reserved.

No part of this book may be reproduced by any means without the written permission of the publisher.

Library of Congress Cataloging-in-Publication Data

Names: Eldridge, Alison, author. | Eldridge, Stephen, author.
Title: Understanding and using microwaves / Alison and Stephen Eldridge.
Description: New York, NY : Enslow Publishing, LLC., [2022] | Series: The electromagnetic spectrum | Includes bibliographical references and index. | Audience: 7-12.
Identifiers: LCCN 2019013436| ISBN 9781978514928 (library bound) | ISBN 1978514921 (library bound) | ISBN 9781978514911 (pbk.) | ISBN 1978514913
 (pbk.)
Subjects: LCSH: Microwaves—Juvenile literature.
Classification: LCC TK7876 .E4126 2022 | DDC 537.5/344—dc23
LC record available at https://lccn.loc.gov/2019013436

Printed in the United States of America

To Our Readers: We have done our best to make sure all websites in this book were active and appropriate when we went to press. However, the author and the publisher have no control over and assume no liability for the material available on those websites or on any websites they may link to. Any comments or suggestions can be sent by email to customerservice@enslow.com.

Photos Credits: Cover © iStockphoto.com/Sirikornt; p. 5 VectorMine/Shutterstock.com; p. 7 Nasky/Shutterstock.com; p. 11 zlikovec/Shutterstock.com; pp. 14, 39 NASA; p. 17 Pasha Gusev/Shutterstock.com; p. 19 Ensuper/Shutterstock.com; p. 22 Universal History Archive/Universal Images Group/Getty Images; p. 24 Pictorial Press Ltd/Alamy Stock Photo; p. 27 Science Museum London/Wikimedia Commons/File: Original cavity magnetron, 1940 (9663811280).jpg/CC BY-SA 2.0; p. 29 Pictorial Parade/Archive Photos/Getty Images; p. 31 Andrey_Popov/Shutterstock.com; p. 32 Avector/Shutterstock.com; p. 34 Ijansempoi/Shutterstock.com; p. 37 Ryan McGinnis/Moment/Getty Images; p. 42 ttsz/iStock/Getty Images; p. 43 National Weather Service/NOAA; pp. 47, 50 NASA/WMAP Science Team; p. 52 Getty Images; cover background, interior pages (faceted color pattern) s_maria/Shutterstock.com; interior pages (wave graphic) MagicMary/Shutterstock.com.

CONTENTS

INTRODUCTION 4

CHAPTER ONE
WHAT ARE MICROWAVES? 7

CHAPTER TWO
WHERE DO MICROWAVES COME FROM? 13

CHAPTER THREE
MICROWAVES THROUGH HISTORY 21

CHAPTER FOUR
MICROWAVES AT HOME 28

CHAPTER FIVE
MICROWAVES AT WORK 36

CHAPTER SIX
MICROWAVES IN SPACE 45

CHAPTER NOTES 54
GLOSSARY 60
FURTHER READING 61
INDEX 62

INTRODUCTION

Sunlight shines through the wet air after a thunderstorm, making a beautiful rainbow. An X-ray machine blasts a human body and records an outline of the bones within. A radio antenna picks up a signal from miles away and turns it into music that blares through a car speaker as a driver travels down the highway. These are all different forms of the same basic concept—electromagnetic radiation.

Electromagnetic radiation is a kind of energy created by electromagnetic fields (fields created by the motion of objects that have a charge, such as electrons). Electromagnetic radiation flows through the universe as waves. It often interacts with other objects as it flows, which is why it can be used by humans for things like communication, medicine, and even eyesight. The many different forms this radiation takes can be described by a simple property called wavelength.

Wavelength, Frequency, and Energy

Imagine a very still pond or pool. Its surface is very smooth and flat. What happens when a stone is dropped into it? Small waves ripple through the water, creating little peaks and valleys. These kinds of waves, known as mechanical waves, work by bumping molecules into each other like dominoes. Any given molecule of water moves very little, but a wave itself can travel across the pond very quickly.

INTRODUCTION

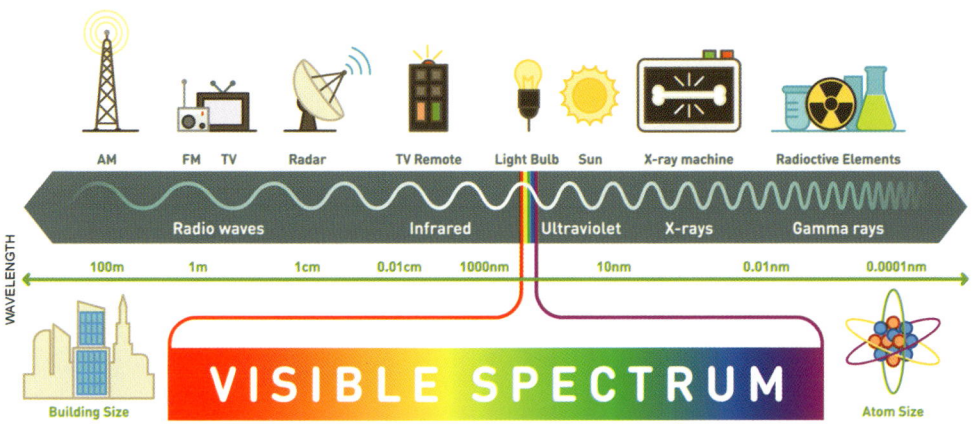

Microwaves have some of the longest wavelengths in the electromagnetic spectrum. In this diagram, they are included with radio waves.

Suppose you want to describe these waves to someone who couldn't see them. One way to describe waves is to talk about the distance between the peaks created as the wave travels. That distance is called a wavelength.

Waves of electromagnetic radiation are somewhat like this. Instead of moving through molecules, the waves move through electromagnetic fields. Because they move through electromagnetic fields, they move at the speed of light. In fact, light itself is a form of electromagnetic radiation! Yet these waves still have peaks and valleys, and people can still measure the length between them to describe a wave.

A related way to describe waves is by their frequency—how many peaks appear in a given time. Smaller wavelengths lead to higher frequencies, because more peaks will fit into a given amount of time when the peaks are closer together.

Electromagnetic waves are thought to be carried by a kind of particle called a photon.[1] A photon is a tiny packet of energy. The amount of energy carried by a photon is related to the wavelength of the electromagnetic wave the photon carries. The shorter the wavelength of an electromagnetic wave, the higher the energy carried by its photon.[2]

The wavelength, frequency, and energy of electromagnetic radiation are what separate the light people see from the energy that cooks food in a microwave oven and the radiation used to sterilize surgical equipment.[3] The infinite array of different wavelengths of electromagnetic radiation is called the electromagnetic spectrum. The spectrum is broken into different regions. Because wavelength, frequency, and energy are so closely related, scientists can classify electromagnetic waves the same way using any of those measurements.

Microwaves are one kind of electromagnetic radiation. They are the electromagnetic waves with one of the longest wavelengths. What exactly are microwaves? How do people encounter them and use them in their daily lives?

WHAT ARE MICROWAVES?

CHAPTER ONE

Microwaves are a kind of electromagnetic radiation. Like all electromagnetic radiation, they can be thought of as waves with a particular wavelength.

Not So Micro

Microwaves are a kind of radio wave. Radio waves are the electromagnetic waves with the longest wavelengths. Usually, microwaves are defined as electromagnetic waves with a wavelength between a tenth of a centimeter

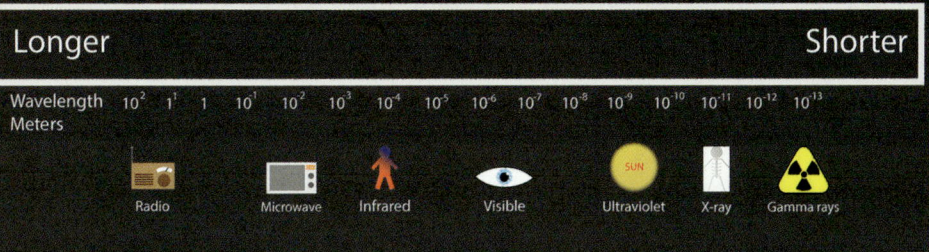

The wavelengths of microwaves are shorter than radio waves and longer than infrared light.

7

UNDERSTANDING AND USING MICROWAVES

and a meter.[1] That means some microwaves have wavelengths that are more than 3 feet long! Like all radio waves, they have much longer wavelengths than visible light, X-rays, and gamma rays.

Microwaves are the radio waves with the smallest wavelengths. Because wavelength is mathematically related to frequency and energy, that means microwaves have relatively high frequencies and energies compared to other radio waves.

There is a lot of variation of microwaves. To talk about them more specifically, they are broken into different "bands." A particular band of microwave radiation represents a section of the electromagnetic spectrum, typically defined by frequency. Microwaves themselves are also a band of high-frequency radio waves.

The Institute of Electrical and Electronics Engineers (or IEEE, pronounced "I-triple-E") is a professional organization

NAMING MICROWAVES

You may know that the prefix "micro-" means small. But microwaves aren't very small compared to other types of electromagnetic waves. In fact, they have the second-biggest wavelength in the electromagnetic spectrum. With wavelengths from about 1 millimeter to 1 meter, they definitely don't extend into the micrometer range either. So how did they get this name? When microwaves were discovered, they were smaller than the other known waves of the time—radio waves. In comparison, they were pretty "micro," and the name stuck.

What Are Microwaves?

that has standardized some bands with letter names. These bands are used to quickly refer to different ranges of frequencies. The different bands are often used for different applications.

Table 1. Bands of microwave energy defined by frequency.

Band Designation	Frequency	Wavelength
L band	1 to 2 GHz	15 to 30 cm
S band	2 to 4 GHz	7.5 to 15 cm
C band	4 to 8 GHz	3.75 to 7.5 cm
X band	8 to 12 GHz	25 to 37.5 mm
Ku band	12 to 18 GHz	16.7 to 25 mm
K band	18 to 26.5 GHz	11.3 to 16.7 mm
Ka band	26.5 to 40 GHz	5.0 to 11.3 mm
Q band	33 to 50 GHz	6.0 to 9.0 mm
U band	40 to 60 GHz	5.0 to 7.5 mm
V band	50 to 75 GHz	4.0 to 6.0 mm
W band	75 to 100 GHz	2.7 to 4.0 mm
F band	90 to 140 GHz	2.1 to 3.3 mm
D band	110 to 170 GHz	1.8 to 2.7 mm

Frequency Matters

The different bands of the spectrum aren't just different sets of numbers. The frequency, wavelength, and energy of different waves directly determine their properties and what they can do.

Lower-frequency radio waves are good for long-distance communication. They can bounce off the atmosphere to travel the globe.[2] Microwaves, however, don't work as well over these great distances. Microwaves are usually used only in communication up to a range of about 30 or 40 miles (48 to 64 kilometers). Higher-frequency microwaves can also be absorbed by particles in the air. Even air that appears clear to human eyes can be opaque in the microwave portion of the spectrum.

Electromagnetic Absorption

Electromagnetic radiation, such as microwaves, can be absorbed by matter. When an electromagnetic wave passes through an object, the atoms in that object may take energy from the wave. If not much energy is absorbed in this way, the object is transparent. If all the energy is absorbed, the object is opaque.

But frequency makes a difference to this absorption.[3] Objects may be opaque to radiation of some frequencies and not others. For example, a pair of sunglasses may be nearly transparent to radiation in the visible spectrum but opaque to harmful ultraviolet radiation. Because different objects absorb different frequencies of radiation, different microwave bands are good for different uses.

What Are Microwaves?

Wavelengths at Work

Low-frequency L-band microwaves can pass through not only the atmosphere and clouds but also through objects like leaves covering the surface of Earth. Forests are transparent to this kind of microwave radiation. That makes this band useful for things like the Global Positioning System (GPS), which guides cars and other traffic. It wouldn't be good if you lost your GPS signal every time you drove through a forest or on a cloudy day. This band is also useful for scientists studying the soil of the planet. It allows them to take measurements even when weather or forests cover the terrain.[4]

Microwaves are useful for GPS because they can pass through objects such as leaves.

The medium-frequency C-band can also penetrate many kinds of weather and atmospheric disturbances. These waves can penetrate clouds, snow, or smoke, making them good for long-distance radio and satellite transmissions.[5] The C, X, and Ku bands are the most common bands used for satellite communications.[6]

Much higher frequency bands, such as the F band, can be absorbed by the atmosphere. This means they aren't as good for long-range communication. However, this makes them more appropriate for uses like Wi-Fi because it allows people in different places to use the same frequencies without interference. They're also useful for scientists studying radiation from the sky—usually at high altitudes where there's less interference from the atmosphere.[7]

WHERE DO MICROWAVES COME FROM?

Microwaves, like all radio waves, are a kind of electromagnetic radiation. Like all electromagnetic radiation, they're produced by changes in electric and magnetic fields. But what does that mean? How does nature produce microwaves? And what are the ways humans have learned to generate them artificially?

Microwaves in nature are often observed in space, most famously from the cosmic microwave background (CMB) radiation. On Earth, scientists and engineers have created a variety of technologies for creating microwaves. These include the vacuum-tube device called a magnetron that powers most microwave ovens.

Naturally Occurring Microwaves

Microwaves, like other electromagnetic radiation, are everywhere. Stars, including the sun, are natural sources of microwaves, just as they're sources of visible light. And many kinds of atoms can produce microwaves

UNDERSTANDING AND USING MICROWAVES

spontaneously, too. When an atom absorbs some kind of energy and becomes excited, it may spontaneously emit a photon to release that excess energy. That photon is often a radio wave in the microwave range.[1]

This can often happen during high-energy events, such as lightning strikes and ball lightning. The massive electrical energy of a lightning bolt can produce many kinds of electromagnetic energy. The most obvious radiation is bright visible light, but lightning strikes are known to also produce microwaves, X-rays, and gamma rays.[2]

Ball lightning is a strange phenomenon in which a ball of electrical energy seems to last much longer than the brief flash of normal lightning. Some scientists believe microwaves are responsible.[3] Their theory is that lightning sometimes can produce such intense microwave radiation that it turns the air around it into plasma. This plasma can form a stable sphere that contains all that powerful radiation in a glowing, crackling ball of energy.[4]

The Juno spacecraft, pictured here in an illustration, detected microwaves from lightning on Jupiter.

14

Where Do Microwaves Come From?

The study of microwaves emitted by lightning has even allowed the observation of lightning on other planets. The Juno spacecraft, launched in 2011, flew close to planet Jupiter and detected powerful bursts of microwaves from lightning. The data showed that Jupiter's lightning is similar to lightning on Earth, even though there are huge differences between the two planets.[5]

The Cosmic Microwave Background Radiation

The cosmic microwave background (CMB) radiation is electromagnetic radiation left over from the Big Bang. It appears throughout the universe in every direction.[6]

REDSHIFT

When a light source is moving away from an observer, the light appears to shift toward the red end of the spectrum. This is called "redshift." It occurs because when the distance between a light source and an observer increases, the frequency of the light waves seems to decrease. The opposite (when a light source is moving toward a point) is called "blueshift."

This doesn't just happen with visible light. Invisible gamma rays can "redshift" all the way past the visible spectrum to become invisible radio waves. Scientists use these concepts to figure out how fast things are moving in space.

Unlike microwaves from stars or lightning, CMB radiation wasn't emitted as microwaves. The observable universe began with the Big Bang 13.8 billion years ago. Over billions of years, the photons produced during the Big Bang have shifted from being extremely high-energy waves to being relatively low-energy microwaves.

How Humans Create Microwaves

People have been creating microwaves artificially for decades. Over the years, engineers have come up with many different designs for devices. These designs fall into two major categories: solid-state devices and vacuum-tube devices.

Solid-State Devices

A solid-state device uses a crystal to help generate or amplify microwaves. The crystal is a semiconductor—a substance that conducts electricity. The most common form for solid-state devices to take is called a transistor.

Transistors are the foundation of almost all modern electronics. Each transistor takes a tiny piece of semiconductor crystal—often the mineral silicon—and uses it to control an electrical current. Transistors can be used to create a device called an oscillator. An oscillator is an electronic circuit that creates a rhythmic, repeating electrical signal.

If that electrical signal is attached to an antenna, a radio transmitter can be made. The movement of this rhythmic electrical signal up and down the antenna creates changing electrical and magnetic fields. When electrical and magnetic fields change,

Transistors can be used to create microwaves.

electromagnetic waves are generated. If the rhythmic change in the fields (called an oscillation) is fast enough, the resulting waves will have a frequency in the microwave band.[7]

There are several other kinds of solid-state devices, but one of the coolest is called the maser. "Maser" is short for Microwave Amplification by Stimulated Emission of Radiation.[8] If that sounds familiar, it may be because a maser is very similar to a laser—Light Amplification by Stimulated Emission of Radiation.

The difference between a maser and a laser is a laser is generally a focused beam of visible light, whereas a maser is a focused beam of microwaves. Though lasers are more famous, masers were actually invented first.

Like transistors, masers produce electrical waves using crystals. But masers work differently. Instead of creating an electrical current through a circuit and antenna, masers excite the atoms in a crystal so they emit photons of a specific frequency.

Masers require very specific conditions. The crystals used in masers are rare. They might be made of rubies and diamonds, for example. And they generally need extremely cold temperatures to run. And extreme does mean extreme! Masers run at temperatures just a few tenths of a degree above absolute zero.[9] That's nearly 460 degrees Fahrenheit (273 degrees Celsius) below zero!

These limitations make it hard to use masers, but they do have some uses in things like radio telescopes and space communication. And believe it or not, scientists have found evidence of naturally occurring masers in space.[10]

Vacuum-Tube Devices

A vacuum tube is a tube made of glass or ceramic that is emptied of all air so the inside is a vacuum. (Sometimes similar devices use special gases in place of vacuums.) A stream of electrons is sent across this vacuum and controlled with electrical or magnetic fields. If a vacuum tube is connected to an antenna or other device for transmitting waves, it can create powerful electromagnetic waves, including microwaves.

Vacuum tubes are an older technology than solid-state devices. Until the late 1950s, they were a basic building block of almost

Where Do Microwaves Come From?

Vacuum tubes can create microwaves if they are connected to a transmitting device.

all electronics. The development of transistors replaced them in most of the items people use every day—computers, radios, and televisions, for example—but vacuum tubes still have their advantages. They are used when there is a need for high power or high frequencies. That makes them very useful for generating microwaves.

Two common types of vacuum-tube devices are called klystrons and magnetrons. In a klystron, high-speed electrons are controlled using electromagnetic fields. Changes in the speed of the electron flow allow for the creation of ultra-high frequency (UHF) microwaves. One use for klystrons is UHF television broadcasting. While a few channels broadcast at very high frequencies (VHF), being able to broadcast in the UHF range allows for more television channel options. Other uses for klystrons include radar and particle accelerators.

Magnetrons use a vacuum tube and an electromagnet to create powerful electromagnetic fields. Attached to an antenna, a magnetron can be used to generate intense microwave energy. Magnetrons have many applications, but you know them best as the devices that power commercial microwave ovens. You probably have a magnetron in your home right now!

MICROWAVES THROUGH HISTORY

Though microwave ovens may be the most famous application of microwaves, other microwave technologies have played a much greater role in shaping human history. The history of microwaves begins with a theory that changed how humans understood the universe itself. It continues today with decades of advancement in communications technology that has shaped the modern world. And it includes a key technology that helped to win the most devastating war in human history.

The Discovery of Microwaves

In the history of science, few figures can be said to have truly revolutionized how people understand the universe. One of these is Scottish physicist James Clerk Maxwell. Maxwell worked with observations of electrical and magnetic lines of force that had been recorded by the pioneering physicist Michael Faraday. Maxwell

UNDERSTANDING AND USING MICROWAVES

used this work by Faraday and others to develop equations that described a new concept: electromagnetism.

Maxwell was the first to describe a theory of electromagnetic radiation, published in 1865.[1] He discovered that electromagnetic forces seemed to travel at a fixed speed—the speed of light. Based on this, he proposed that light and electromagnetism were related. Maxwell's work unified electricity, magnetism, and light, changing how humans thought about the universe forever.

Maxwell's theory led to more revolutionary research in electromagnetism. The first person to conclusively demonstrate that Maxwell's theories were correct was the German physicist Heinrich Hertz.[2] In the late 1880s, Hertz used Maxwell's theories to generate electromagnetic waves—including microwaves. His experiments confirmed that electromagnetic disturbances moved in waves, as light does, at the same speed as light. He

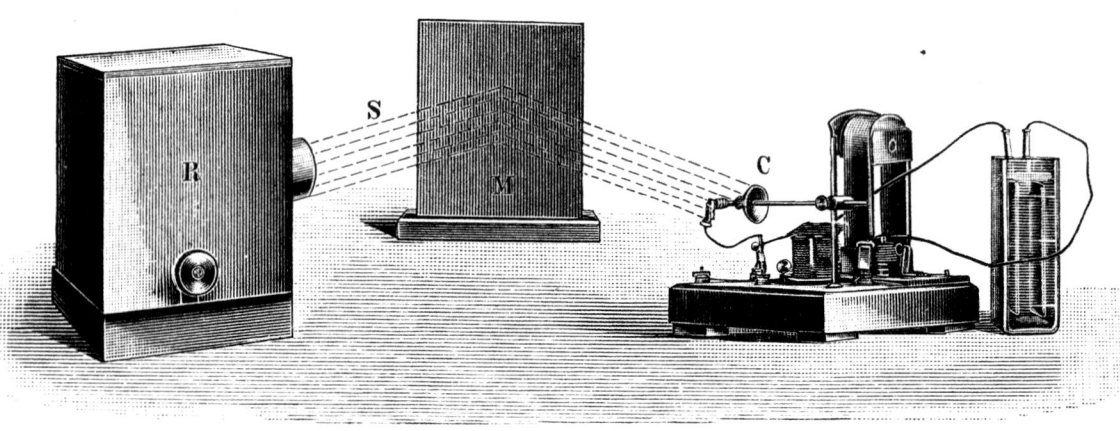

Heinrich Hertz's work included reflecting electromagnetic waves. The resonator (R) sends out waves (S), which are reflected by a mirror (M) and received by another resonator (C).

also confirmed they could be reflected and refracted in the same way as light.

Hertz was not the first person to generate electromagnetic waves. An inventor named David Hughes managed that feat several years before Hertz.[3] However, Hughes's work was mostly ignored at the time, and he didn't work on the key electromagnetic principles that Hertz proved in his work.

With electromagnetic waves understood for the first time, the race was on to find applications for them. One early pioneer in the use of microwaves was a biologist. Jagadish Chandra Bose was an Indian scientist who worked mostly with plants. But in the 1890s, he set up a laboratory and conducted experiments with electromagnetic waves. He patented his own techniques for detecting electromagnetic radiation, including using crystals in early solid-state devices. Similar technology wouldn't become widespread for decades. Bose was at least sixty years ahead of his time.[4]

REFRACTION

Refraction is a concept in physics that describes how a wave changes in direction when it passes through a material because of its change in speed. Waves always want to travel the fastest way possible, which is usually in a straight line. But certain mediums make them slow down. To continue traveling the fastest path, they bend. You can see this if you look at a straw in a glass of water. Light waves travel faster through the air than they do through water. The straw appears bent because the light waves bend in the water.

Jagadish Chandra Bose contributed to the fields of physics, biology, and botany.

Bose was also ahead when it came to the race to use electromagnetism for communication at a distance. While it was the Italian inventor Guglielmo Marconi who would eventually become known as the key pioneer of radio, Bose actually conducted a successful public exhibition to send and receive microwaves at a distance two years before Marconi's first successful wireless signaling experiment. Rather than sending a message in words, however, Bose's demonstration was more concrete. He used microwaves to ring a bell—and also to explode some gunpowder![5]

However, Marconi's results proved more influential. Radio communication focused for many years on relatively long wavelengths that could travel for many miles. Microwaves were mostly neglected for decades. Then in the 1930s, a revolutionary invention created a new interest in microwaves. That invention was radar.

Radar and the Second World War

Radar (short for *Ra*dio *D*etection *a*nd *R*anging) is a method of using electromagnetic waves to detect faraway objects and determine their distance. Many objects, such as clouds, that are opaque to visible light are transparent to some microwave frequencies. That means that radar using microwaves can detect objects like airplanes from a great distance away even in cloudy conditions. (Similar technology using visible light is known as lidar.)

The possibility of using electromagnetic radiation in this way had been around for decades before it was developed. Heinrich Hertz had provided most of the necessary principles by demonstrating that electromagnetic waves could be reflected by metallic objects. In 1904, a German engineer named Christian Hülsmeyer patented a device for detecting obstacles to ships.[6] However, there was little interest in the device, and radio detection technology was largely set aside.

In the 1930s, a different technology created a very urgent need for effective radar. That technology was the kind of airplane known as a bomber. The newly developed ability to send long-range planes to drop bombs on cities led at least eight different countries to independently develop some kind of radar technology during the 1930s.

When World War II broke out in 1939, these countries found themselves on different sides of the conflict. The countries that would become known as the Allied powers—Britain, France, the United States, and the Soviet Union—all had some kind of radar system. However, the Axis powers of Germany, Italy, and Japan also possessed radar. The eighth country to possess radar technology at the time was the Netherlands. They were officially neutral in the conflict, though Germany eventually invaded them anyway.

In 1939, Nazi Germany had more advanced radar technology than any other nation.[7] However, by 1940 their early military successes led them to believe that further development of radar wasn't very important. Improving radar systems wasn't given a high priority. This decision gave their enemies, the Allied powers, a chance to catch up—and then surpass them.

Early radar systems had used relatively low frequencies. These radio waves could travel great distances but had many disadvantages. Their long wavelengths made it more difficult to determine objects' positions precisely. And they couldn't reliably penetrate disturbances in the atmosphere. Scientists knew greater frequencies were needed to make radar more effective, but no one had yet figured out how to make microwave radar work.

That changed in late 1939, when British scientists made new advances in magnetron technology. They shared their new magnetrons with the United States in 1940.[8] At the Massachusetts Institute of Technology, researchers used magnetron technology to create a new generation of radar devices that operated in the microwave range of frequencies. These devices used microwaves to detect objects more precisely, even in poor atmospheric conditions. Some of them were small enough to be carried on planes, giving powerful tools to Allied pilots. Planes could even find and attack submerged submarines using microwave radar!

The race to build more effective radar technology drove rapid advancement of the technology during the war. This new technology changed the face of warfare and had other impacts

Microwaves Through History

Magnetron advancements made by British scientists in the late 1930 and early 1940s had a huge impact on World War II.

as well. The technological advancements during this period laid the groundwork for the development of transistors as well as the more advanced microwave communication that makes modern communications technology possible.

CHAPTER FOUR
MICROWAVES AT HOME

The advances in magnetron technology during World War II led to many more breakthroughs in the following decades. Today, microwaves and the machines that generate them are all around. Many people have a microwave oven in their home. But it might be surprising to know that microwaves do much more each day than just cook food. They are a vital part of the way people communicate.

Microwave Ovens

Microwave ovens are everywhere. They're in many homes and commercial kitchens. But how do they actually work? Are they dangerous? And why aren't you supposed to put metal in the microwave anyway?

Microwave ovens were developed after World War II. They were made possible by the new and powerful magnetrons invented at the time. In 1946, a researcher named Percy L. Spencer was working with magnetrons for the giant industrial company Raytheon. Spencer redesigned magnetrons so they could be produced more

Microwaves at Home

quickly. One day, he was standing near an active magnetron and noticed that some chocolate he had in his pocket had warmed up and melted.[1]

Spencer had discovered a principle called radiant heating. When electromagnetic radiation interacts with an object, it loses some amount of energy. That energy is absorbed by the object. That additional energy makes the object warmer. If you've ever noticed that sunlight feels warm, you've experienced radiant heating.

Spencer's further experiments with heating eggs and popping popcorn led to the eventual development of Raytheon's Radarange, the first microwave oven.[2] "Radarange" came from a combination of the word "radar" (the most famous use of radiation at the time) and the word "range" (as in a stove top). In the 1950s, the Radarange was used primarily for commercial purposes—in industrial kitchens, not home kitchens. But by 1967, prices had dropped far enough that some homeowners could afford to buy them.[3]

This chef is using a Radarange, the first type of microwave oven.

Are Microwave Ovens Safe?

As long as microwave ovens have been around, people have raised questions about their safety. Radiation can be dangerous, so having a magnetron spewing radiation in your home might sound a little scary! So are microwaves really safe? Yes, but there are some reasons to be cautious.

The most dangerous kind of radiation is called ionizing radiation. Ionizing radiation is radiation that's powerful enough to change the charge of atoms, including the atoms in our bodies. Nuclear radiation, like that from radioactive elements, is often dangerous ionizing radiation. Exposure to that radiation can damage your internal organs or increase your risk of cancer.

Microwaves, however, are non-ionizing radiation. Like other radio waves, they do not carry enough energy to change the charge of atoms in the human body. They will generally not cause the same kinds of problems as ionizing radiation.

However, microwave radiation may still carry risks. Intense microwave radiation like that used to cook food can also heat up the human body. Uncontrolled, this can cause burns or damage to sensitive organs such as the eyes.[4] Because of this, microwave ovens are designed so that when closed they allow virtually no radiation to escape. They're also designed so they cannot operate unless the door is fully closed. However, damage to microwave ovens can still lead to radiation leaks—so treat your microwave ovens gently.

Microwave Safety

A microwave oven uses a magnetron to turn electrical energy from your wall socket into powerful microwave radiation that cooks

Microwaves at Home

Microwave radiation can be dangerous, but microwave ovens are designed to be safe for humans to use.

your food. The walls and door of the oven reflect microwaves like a mirror so that the radiation bounces around within the microwave and is absorbed by the food inside. Molecules in the food heat up, and the food cooks.[5]

It sounds simple, but it can be a little more complicated. You might have noticed that food in a microwave is often extremely hot on the outside, but ice-cold on the inside. You might have heard that some plates and containers aren't "microwave safe."

UNDERSTANDING AND USING MICROWAVES

And you might be really sick of being told to never, ever put metal in the microwave. And you might have wondered: Why?

All these questions can be answered by understanding how microwave energy is absorbed—or not absorbed.

When food is heated by a microwave oven, it is struck by microwave radiation. But microwave radiation doesn't penetrate very far through food. Water, sugar, and fat in food are pretty good at absorbing microwaves, so while the outside of the food heats up quickly, the inside heats much more slowly. In fact, generally it isn't the microwaves themselves that heat the inside of food. It's the hot outside of the food that heats the inside.

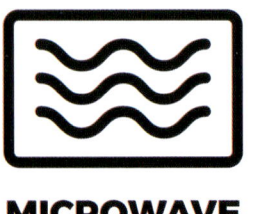

MICROWAVE   **MICROWAVE OVEN SAFE**   **MICROWAVE OVEN SAFE**

Some plastics have symbols like these to show they're microwave safe, or able to be used in a microwave.

This is why to properly heat food, it's best to stir it if possible. If that's not possible, leaving food in the microwave for a minute or two after heating can help the outside of the food cool down and warm up the inside.

Because not all molecules absorb microwave radiation equally, some materials are more or less safe to put in a microwave. Plastics should never be microwaved unless they specifically say they are microwave safe. Some plastics heat up in a microwave just like food. They can melt, contaminating the food or causing burns when touched. Some plastics may even introduce chemicals into the food without being noticeably hot![6] Plates and dishes that aren't plastic may absorb microwaves and become extremely hot to touch, causing burns.

WHY CAN'T YOU PUT METAL IN A MICROWAVE?

The inside of your microwave oven is made of metal, but putting metal objects in a microwave oven can still be dangerous. This is because metal reflects the waves and bounces them around inside the microwave. That's how the waves heat your food. But if a metal object inside the microwave reflects too much, it can cause an arc of electricity, like a tiny lightning bolt. It can also cause damage to the inside of your microwave. If the inside of your microwave gets damaged enough, it won't work anymore. And if the metal reflects the waves away from your food, your food won't get heated anyway.

UNDERSTANDING AND USING MICROWAVES

Microwave Communication

Microwaves don't just cook your food. They're also a key part of the networks that connect you to television, telephones, and the internet. If you have Wi-Fi, your connection depends on microwave radiation. If you use a cell phone, your phone uses microwaves to connect to your cellular carrier network. And if you watch broadcast television, you may be picking up signals on a network of thousands of microwave towers connecting across the United States.

Wi-Fi is how most wireless computers connect to the internet. If you have Wi-Fi in your home, a device called a router somewhere in or near your home transmits a microwave signal that your computer or other device can receive. Your device will also transmit a microwave signal that the router receives. This router connects your device to your internet service provider's network, and you get internet access.

One oddity of Wi-Fi is that the signal it uses is in the same

A Wi-Fi router works by transmitting and receiving microwave signals.

34

Microwaves at Home

frequency range that microwave ovens use—2.4 gigahertz, or 2.4 billion cycles per second. Because of that, even a tiny amount of microwave radiation leaking from your microwave oven can cause interference in a Wi-Fi signal.[7] If you notice that your internet connection goes down every time you turn on the microwave oven, it might be time for a new microwave oven.

Cell phones usually work on different frequencies, so there's little interference between a cellular signal and a Wi-Fi signal.[8] Cell phone signals also usually travel much farther. While Wi-Fi routers are usually found in homes and businesses, cell phone towers are not so common. The power of cell phone microwave radiation has led some people to be concerned about the amount of radiation cell phones emit. Cell phone radiation, like other microwaves, is not ionizing radiation. And so far the National Cancer Institute has found no consistent evidence that cell phones can increase cancer risk, or that they cause significant heating in the body.[9] However, because microwaves are all around us, scientists continue to study them to assess their safety.

Another kind of microwave that's all around us is television broadcast signals. Standard television broadcasts are transmitted using radio waves, including both the VHF and UHF bands of the electromagnetic spectrum. UHF waves are sometimes considered microwaves, though in broadcasting they are often just called radio waves. These signals are shared from broadcasters through a network of "repeater" stations that receive television signals and repeat them, extending their broadcast range. Though today most television viewing is done via cable or the internet, these networks still exist and can be tuned into for the price of a simple antenna.

MICROWAVES AT WORK

Microwaves aren't just useful around the home. They are an important part of many industries, from food preparation to manufacturing to weather forecasting. And technology for generating and controlling microwaves continues to advance.

Microwaves in Industry

Microwave radiation works in most industries very similarly to how it works in a microwave oven—by heating things up. But cooking food isn't the only reason to use microwaves for heat. They actually have a lot of advantages over conventional heating methods.

Industrial processes often used a method of heating called surface heating. This is essentially the same method you might use to boil a pot of water on a stove. A liquid or semisolid is poured into a container, and the surfaces of that container are heated up. But this method has some drawbacks. It's not very efficient, and a lot of heat is lost in the process. It's hard to heat up a container evenly, so some parts of the substance being heated might burn or not be heated enough. It's

Microwaves at Work

Doppler radar used by this tornado truck helps forecast weather.

also slow to try to heat a large amount of liquid by heating up the edges.

Microwaves can be used in a different process called volumetric heating. In volumetric heating, the entire volume of a substance is heated at the same time. The substance flows through the heating chamber and is heated very quickly by microwave radiation. The electromagnetic radiation is able to heat evenly throughout the substance all at once. Unlike a pot on a stove, microwaves don't need time to heat up or cool down. They can be turned on and off instantly.

This kind of heating does have some drawbacks. Even though it's possible to heat a whole volume at once, it can still be difficult to heat evenly with microwaves. And microwaves can't penetrate too deeply into substances. That limits how much can be heated at a time. However, the shorter heating time and lower energy needed usually outweigh these drawbacks.

Microwave heating is used to rapidly dry objects. A product or part might be painted and the paint dried quickly and evenly with microwave radiation. Microwaves are also used for curing. Curing is a process by which a substance is dried and hardened during production. Objects made of rubber, concrete, or plastic may be cured to ensure they're strong and hard enough. This kind of drying and curing leads to fewer product defects with less time and energy use. Microwaves can also apply heat more selectively than traditional methods, so that one part of an object is rapidly dried or cured while another stays relatively cool.

Developing Microwave Tech

As microwave technology becomes more advanced, opportunities for other uses arise. Today, scientists are working on developing ideas around microwave energy transfer—and also around microwave weapons.

Experiments in transmitting energy using microwaves have been occurring since at least 1964, when scientists managed to power a small helicopter using microwaves.[1] The idea is that a microwave transmitter can be used to send microwave radiation to a machine with a receiver. A device called a rectifier attached to the receiver converts the microwave radiation into usable power.

Microwaves at Work

Scientists are trying to develop ways to transfer power from space using microwave transmissions. That may involve leaving tech on the moon, like this lunar module.

An antenna with a rectifier is often called a rectifying antenna or rectenna. Though the helicopter worked, it's been difficult to achieve good results at large scales using this technology.

Still, some ideas for microwave power transmission have been very big. David Criswell, a scientist at the University of Houston, is one of several people to propose using microwave transmissions from space to supply power to Earth. In Criswell's plan, a solar power station would be built on the moon. This station would then beam power from the moon to tens of thousands of receivers on Earth. This process would involve a network of satellites stretching around the planet, beaming energy to one another so the whole Earth could be powered no matter what time of day it was.[2]

Unfortunately, building and maintaining these kinds of stations on the moon would require an enormous amount of time and money. And the technology to transmit energy at that scale is still theoretical. But it could be that one day power stations on the moon will beam power toward Earth all day and all night.

That thought gets a little scarier when you know that some scientists have worked on developing microwave weapons. However, one of the main advantages of microwave weapons is they can be nonlethal. The Active Denial System (ADS) is a project the United States military funded to create a nonlethal microwave weapons system.[3]

ADS is a kind of directed-energy weapon, a weapon that uses electromagnetic energy instead of a physical object, like a bullet or missile. Most nonlethal weapons that are used to control crowds or secure checkpoints use objects, like beanbags, to injure people without killing them. However, even

Microwaves at Work

RADAR GUNS

Police know when to pull someone over for going past the speed limit because they have special devices called radar guns that help them test how fast a car is moving. Radar guns send out radio waves, which bounce off the car and echo back. The radar gun can tell how fast the car is going because of something called the Doppler effect. If both the gun and the car were standing still, the frequency of the waves would always be the same. But when the car moves toward the gun, thanks to the Doppler effect, the frequency increases. The radar gun measures this change in frequency to tell how fast the car is going.

with these methods, accidents can happen and deaths are possible. The ADS system uses microwaves to heat the water in a person's skin, causing intense pain with very little lasting damage. It lowers the chance of a serious injury or death during nonlethal operations.[4]

ADS prototypes exist but aren't yet widely used. In the future, it's possible that we may see many dangerous weapons replaced with safer microwave variants.

Advances in Radar

Since its early military days, radar has become more and more important in our society. It's used by air traffic controllers to track planes in the sky and on the ground. It's used by scientists mapping the surface of other worlds, as well as our own. And

UNDERSTANDING AND USING MICROWAVES

every day it helps millions of people decide whether or not to take an umbrella with them when they leave their home.

One of the most significant advances in radar since World War II is the development of Doppler radar for use in meteorology. Since the 1950s, the United States government and others have used microwaves to track storms and help predict the weather.

The principles of Doppler radar have existed for many years. In 1842, the Austrian physicist Christian Doppler first explained the Doppler effect.[5] The Doppler effect is simply the way the frequency of a wave appears to change due to relative motion.

You may have noticed that sometimes when an ambulance is approaching, its siren sounds very high pitched until it passes you and seems to get lower in pitch. This is because as the

Doppler effect

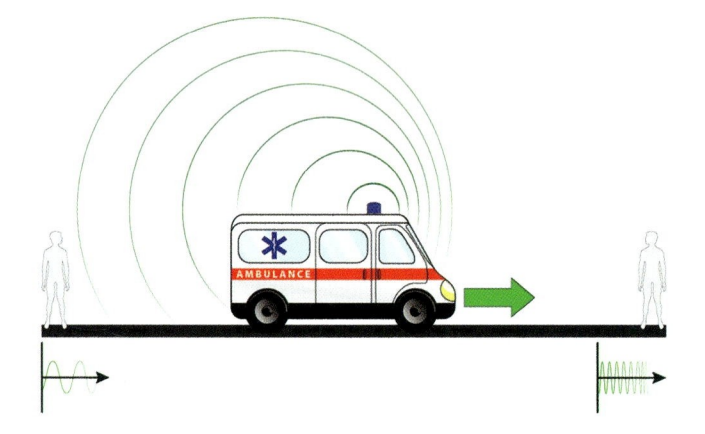

The Doppler effect explains why an ambulance's siren sounds more high pitched until it passes you.

Microwaves at Work

ambulance moves toward you, it is traveling in the same direction as the sound waves you're hearing. That means the sound waves will arrive at your location closer together than they would if the ambulance were stationary. When the ambulance passes you, the reverse is true. Because the ambulance is moving in the opposite direction from the sound waves that are reaching you, the distance between the waves is increased.

The same thing is true with all kinds of waves. Imagine standing in a still pool of water and a rock was dropped in the center. The waves from the rock would ripple toward you at a certain frequency. But if you started to swim toward the rock, you would encounter each wave more quickly. Your motion would affect the frequency of the waves you observed. Electromagnetic waves are no exception. Doppler radar is used to tell not only where an object is but how it is moving.

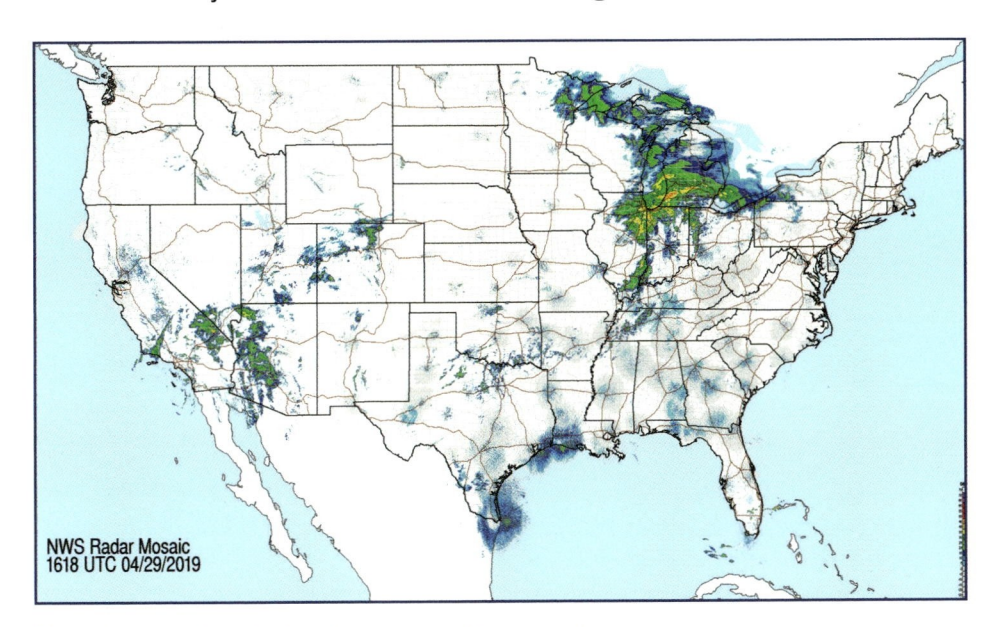

Doppler radar helps forecast the weather.

When a radar wave is transmitted, the radar device listens for electromagnetic "echoes" from objects in the wave's path. With Doppler radar, the difference between the wavelength of the original pulse and the wavelength of the echo is used to calculate the motion of the object.[6]

Today, Doppler radar used for meteorology is capable of picking out snow, rain, or hail in high resolution and determining the direction it is moving. The National Weather Service (NWS) has a Doppler radar program that uses repeated radar pulses at different angles to generate a three-dimensional model of the atmosphere around the radar, called a volume coverage pattern. With this technology, the NWS can get a full model of a storm, including its motion, updated every four to six minutes![7]

MICROWAVES IN SPACE

Microwaves are best known for their use in our day-to-day lives. But they've also helped people to understand some of the biggest and most fundamental forces of the universe. Microwaves are integral to understanding time and space. They help with both observing the history of the universe and deciding where the future might take us.

Microwaves and the Origin of the Universe

In 1965, two researchers named Arno Penzias and Robert Wilson were building a radio receiver. They noticed a strange signal the receiver was picking up. The signal appeared to be coming from every direction, as if there was a microwave signal coming from everywhere in the sky at once.[1]

Meanwhile, Robert Dicke and a team of researchers at Princeton University were looking for evidence of the Big Bang. A few years earlier, a cosmologist named Ralph Alpher had been working on the Big Bang theory.

He predicted that if their theories were correct, there should be radiation permeating the universe left over from the early days of the universe. Dicke's team was searching for evidence of this radiation.

With Penzias and Wilson's discovery, Dicke's team believed they had found what they were looking for. The two researchers had stumbled across something now called the cosmic microwave background (CMB) radiation.[2]

The CMB radiation is a remnant of the Big Bang, the event that set the universe into motion 13.8 billion years ago.[3] This explosive moment of creation filled the universe with energy. The early universe was so hot that even atoms couldn't exist. Particles such as protons and electrons were broken apart and scattered. This kind of hot stream of charged particles is called plasma. These charged particles were opaque to electromagnetic radiation, scattering photons the way a cloud scatters light. It was incredibly dense and incredibly hot.

This early state of the universe lasted less than about 400,000 years. That's a long time to us, but the blink of an eye to the universe. In that time, the universe cooled enough for atoms to form. With the highly charged plasma gone, electromagnetic radiation in the form of photons could move around freely. This was the origin of the CMB—those photons beginning to radiate through the universe. Scientists call the last opaque plasma state that scattered the CMB radiation the "surface of last scattering."[4] That's the picture of the universe the CMB radiation shows us today.

Over billions of years, the universe has expanded and cooled. About 380,000 years after the Big Bang, the temperature was

Microwaves in Space

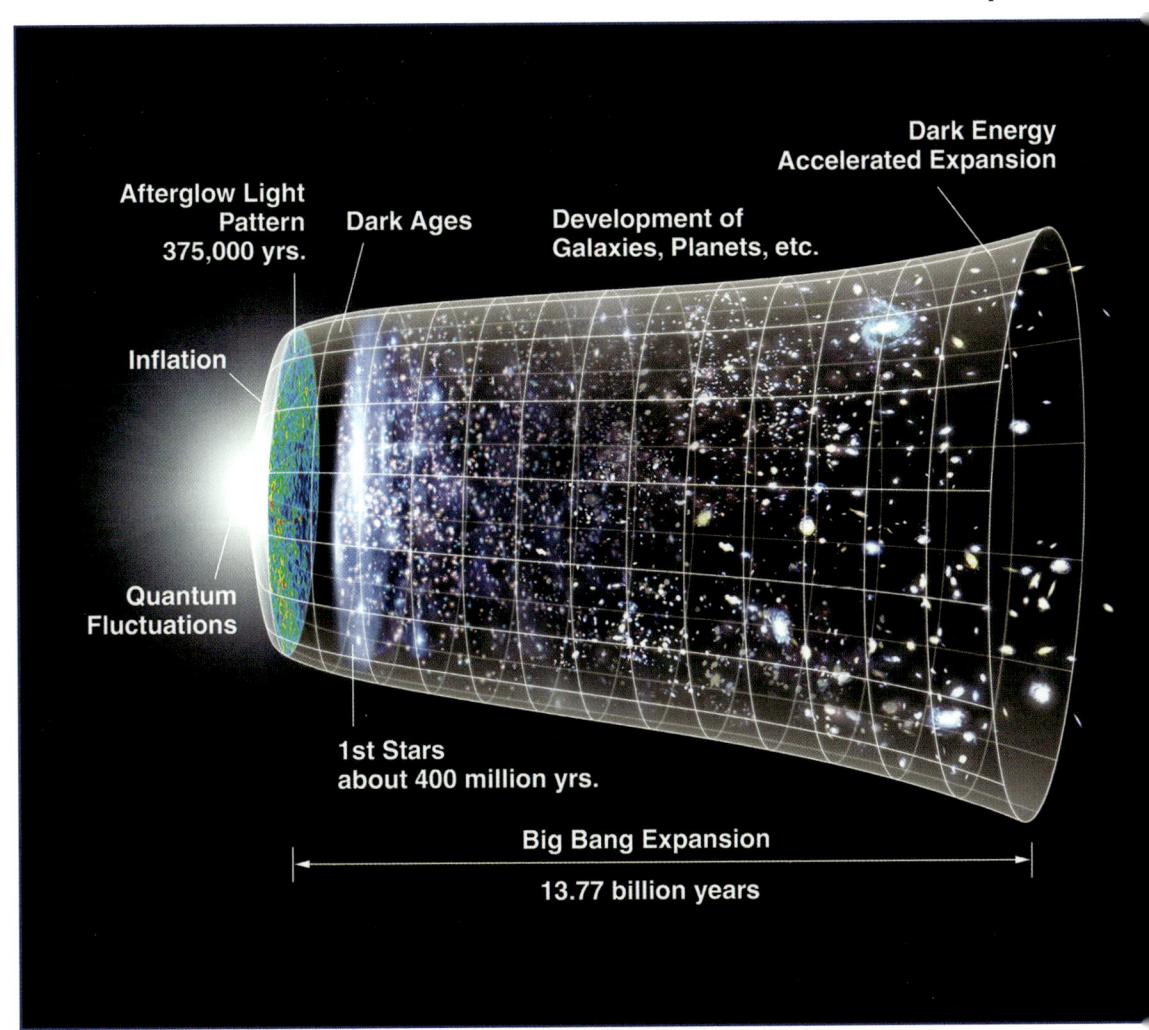

Afterglow Light Pattern 375,000 yrs.
Dark Ages
Development of Galaxies, Planets, etc.
Dark Energy Accelerated Expansion
Inflation
Quantum Fluctuations
1st Stars about 400 million yrs.
Big Bang Expansion
13.77 billion years

This illustration shows how the universe has expanded since the Big Bang. Research into the CMB radiation has helped confirm theories about how this happened.

about 273 million degrees Celsius. The universe was also only about one hundred millionth of its size today. Over thirteen billion years later, the temperature of the CMB throughout the universe today is about 3 degrees above absolute zero.[5]

UNDERSTANDING AND USING MICROWAVES

BACKGROUND RADIATION

There's radiation around you everywhere you go. About half of it is from natural sources, and the other half is from human-made sources. Some natural radiation comes from space—from the sun and other stars—and some of it comes from Earth. Some of it even comes from human bodies. Human-made radiation comes from X-rays, televisions, and smoke detectors, among other sources. Some human-made radiation has also come from nuclear fallout—the aftermath of nuclear reactor accidents or nuclear weapons testing. However, all this radiation still adds up to a very small amount. This sort of everyday radiation exposure has not been shown to have a negative effect on human health.

The electromagnetic radiation released has also undergone redshift due to how much the universe have expanded. It has changed from ultra-powerful gamma rays to lower-frequency microwaves. These microwaves were what Penzias and Wilson heard on their receiver.[6]

Continued research on the CMB radiation has helped confirm theories about the Big Bang. It's also provided some surprises. These surprises have led to an understanding of the structure of the universe and how galaxies form. They've helped scientists pin down the age of the universe and the stars. And they continue to teach us about some of the great mysteries facing science today, like dark matter and dark energy.

Microwaves in Satellites

Not all the microwave radiation flowing through space is a natural remnant of the early universe. Some of it is the result of human activity. People use satellites that transmit and receive microwaves every day. These satellites help with communication, studies of Earth, and navigation.

Satellite Communication

Today, satellites are a vital part of how people communicate with each other. Approximately twenty thousand communication satellites orbit Earth today.[7] Satellites are used for television, telephones, internet communications, and more.

Satellite communication begins on the ground. A signal from Earth, such as a radio broadcast, is sent to a ground station. The ground station creates a satellite "uplink." This means it establishes communication with a satellite orbiting above the station. The satellite receives this signal. The signal is amplified and then transmitted back to Earth. There it is picked up by another receiver—for instance, a satellite radio in a car.[8]

The Global Positioning System (GPS)

The Global Positioning System was originally a United States military project, but today this network of navigation satellites helps travelers across the world get where they're going. There are about thirty GPS satellites, each orbiting Earth about 12,000 miles (19,000 km) above us.[9]

UNDERSTANDING AND USING MICROWAVES

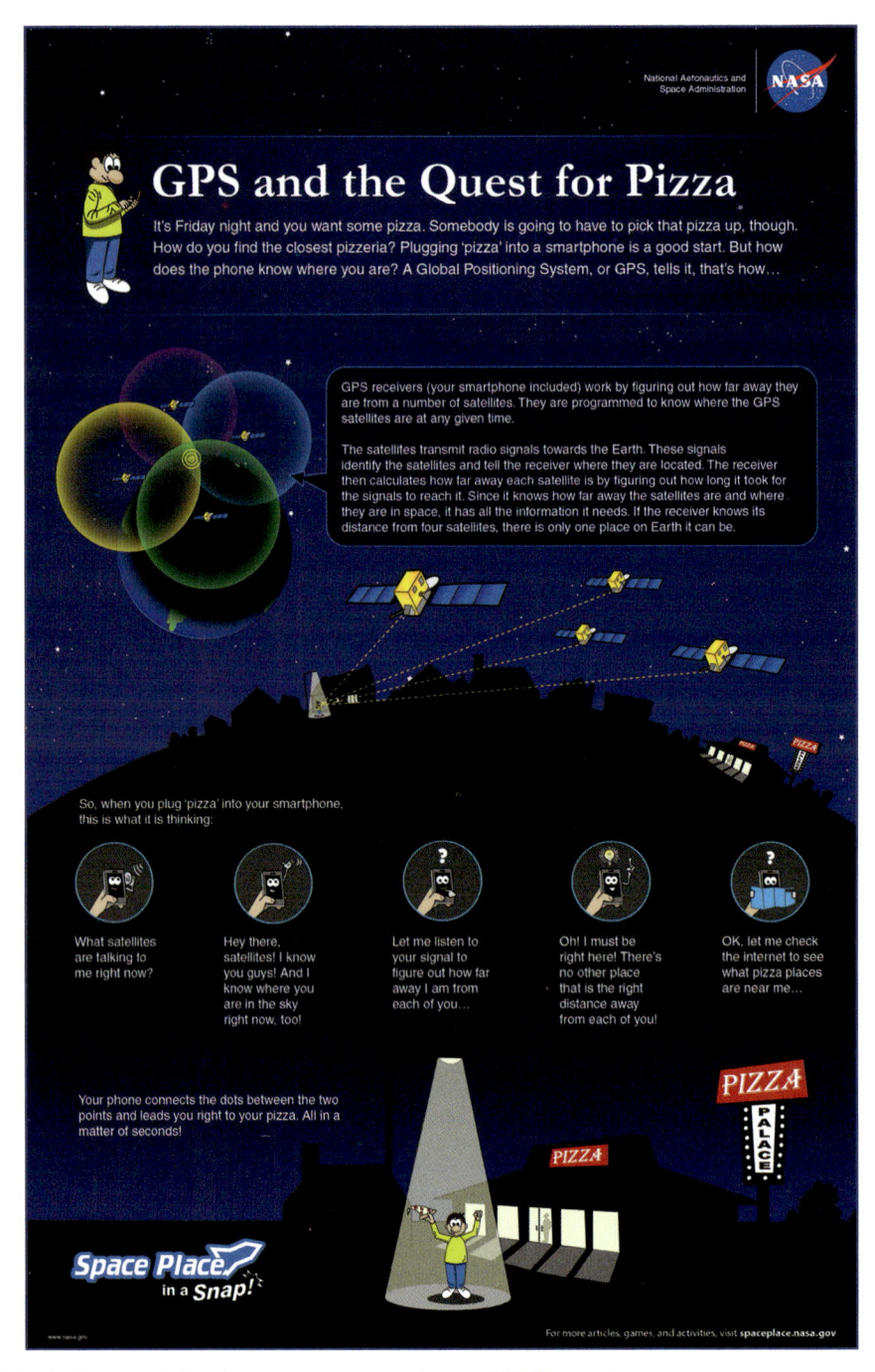

This infographic demonstrates how GPS works.

No matter where you are on Earth, at least four GPS satellites are visible to you at any given time.[10] You may not be able to see them with your naked eyes, but you will have a line of sight to them. This means if you have a GPS device, you can send and receive signals with at least four satellites at a time.

A GPS satellite sends out a microwave signal containing the precise time and the satellite's position. Like all electromagnetic radiation, this signal travels at the speed of light. When your device receives the signal, it can use the time it took the signal to reach you to determine how far you are from the satellite. By combining data from several satellites, it can determine where you are on the planet very precisely.[11]

Studying Our Planet

Doppler radar isn't the only way scientists use microwaves to study Earth. "Microwave remote sensing" is a term used for the study of objects at a distance using microwaves. Scientists use a number of microwave devices mounted on radars to study the planet this way.

A microwave radiometer is a sensor that picks up microwave radiation. Scientists can use it to detect microwave radiation emitted naturally by Earth. It can help measure how much water is in the atmosphere. A radiometer is a kind of "passive remote sensing," because it does not send out its own microwave pulses, it only measures existing microwaves.

A radar altimeter is a kind of radar device. Instead of finding objects in the sky, it sends radar pulses from a satellite toward

UNDERSTANDING AND USING MICROWAVES

Earth. The time it takes the pulses to echo back to the satellite tells the altimeter the elevation of the land it is passing over. An altimeter is a kind of "active remote sensing." It actively emits microwaves and studies the return signals.

A wind scatterometer also sends out a pulse of microwaves, but instead of measuring distance it measures wind speed. Still ocean waters reflect microwaves differently than choppy ocean caused by wind. By measuring the signal reflected by the ocean, scientists can work out the wind speed over the ocean.

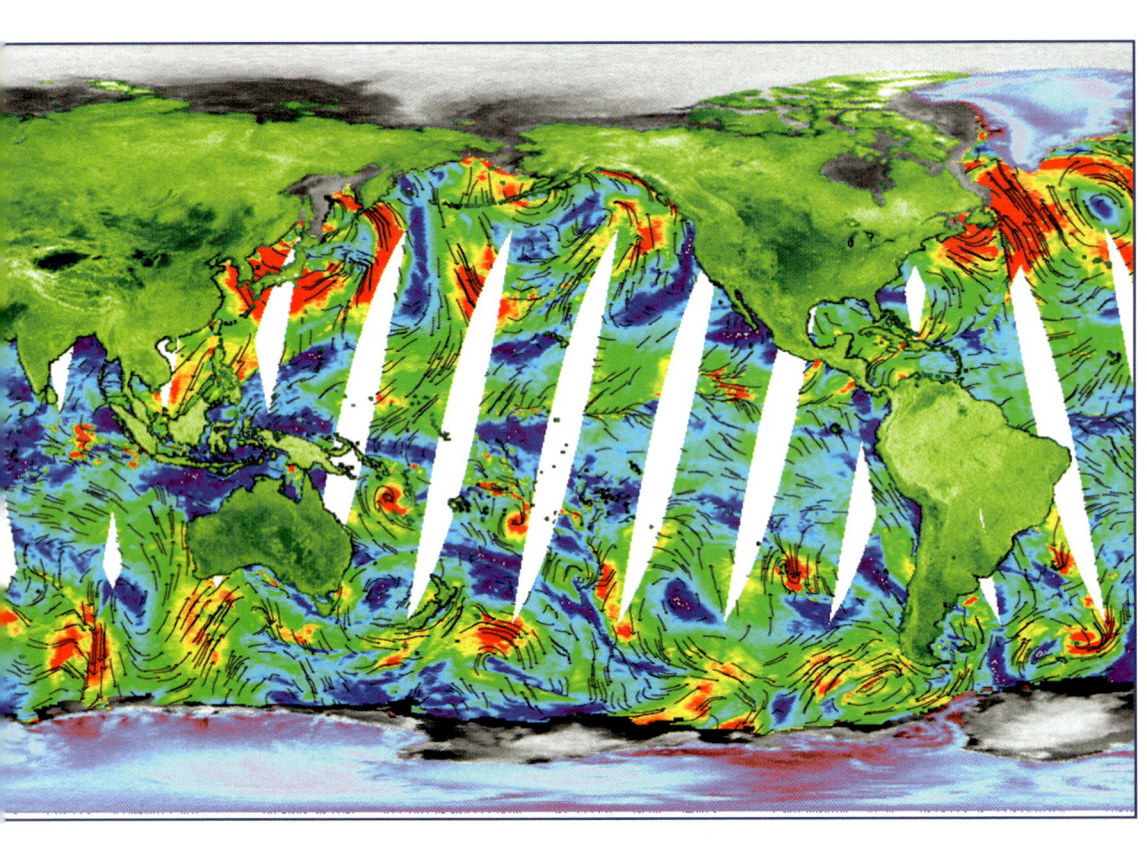

This data collected from a wind scatterometer shows sea winds and ice flow.

Microwaves in Space

  The ability of microwaves to penetrate cloud cover means that tools like these can be used even when it is very stormy. They're often used to understand the threat posed by storms such as hurricanes as they travel across the ocean toward land.

  Microwaves may seem mundane, something used every day to heat up TV dinners and frozen burritos. But in fact they help us connect to the world and learn about not only our world but also the whole universe beyond.

CHAPTER NOTES

INTRODUCTION

1. Encyclopaedia Britannica, "Photon," https://www.britannica.com/science/photon (accessed March 13, 2019).
2. NASA Science, "Anatomy of an Electromagnetic Wave," https://science.nasa.gov/ems/02_anatomy (accessed March 13, 2019).
3. NASA Science, "Anatomy of an Electromagnetic Wave."

CHAPTER 1
WHAT ARE MICROWAVES?

1. Anne Marie Helmenstine, "Microwave Radiation Definition," https://www.thoughtco.com/microwave-radiation-definition-4145800 (accessed March 13, 2019).
2. Helmenstine, "Microwave Radiation Definition."
3. Encyclopaedia Britannica, "Electromagnetic Radiation," https://www.britannica.com/science/electromagnetic-radiation/The-electromagnetic-spectrum (accessed March 13, 2019).
4. NASA Science, "Microwaves," https://science.nasa.gov/ems/06_microwaves (accessed March 13, 2019).
5. Helmenstine, "Microwave Radiation Definition."
6. Helmenstine, "Microwave Radiation Definition."
7. NASA, "Imagine the Universe!" https://imagine.gsfc.nasa.gov/science/toolbox/emspectrum_observatories1.html (accessed March 13, 2019).

CHAPTER 2
WHERE DO MICROWAVES COME FROM?

1. Gravity Probe B, "What Is a MASER?" https://einstein.stanford.edu/content/faqs/maser.html (accessed March 13, 2019).
2. HPS, "Answer to Question #10893 Submitted to 'Ask the Experts,'" https://hps.org/publicinformation/ate/q10893.html (accessed March 13, 2019).
3. *Nature*, "Relativistic-Microwave Theory of Ball Lightning," https://www.nature.com/articles/srep28263 (accessed March 13, 2019).
4. *Nature*, "Relativistic-Microwave Theory of Ball Lightning."
5. "Juno Solves 39-Year-Old Mystery of Jupiter Lightning," https://www.nasa.gov/feature/jpl/juno-solves-39-year-old-mystery-of-jupiter-lightning (accessed March 13, 2019).
6. Space.com, "Cosmic Microwave Background: Remnant of the Big Bang," https://www.space.com/33892-cosmic-microwave-background.html (accessed March 13, 2019).
7. Center for Cosmological Physics, "Radio Wave Basics," https://kicp.uchicago.edu/education/explorers/2002summer-YERKES/pdfs-sum02/background.pdf (accessed March 13, 2019).
8. Gravity Probe B, "What Is a MASER?"
9. Science Alert, "Scientists Just Made the World's First Diamond Maser That Operates at Room Temperature," https://www.sciencealert.com/maser-microwave-diamond-sapphire-room-temperature-solid-state (accessed March 13, 2019).
10. Gravity Probe B, "What Is a MASER?"

CHAPTER 3
MICROWAVES THROUGH HISTORY

1. D. T. Emerson, "The Work of Jagadis Chandra Bose: 100 Years of MM-Wave Research," https://www.cv.nrao.edu/~demerson/bose/bose.html (accessed March 13, 2019).
2. P. S. Ramsay, "Heinrich Hertz, the Father of Frequency," https://www.ncbi.nlm.nih.gov/pubmed/23682537 (accessed March 13, 2019).
3. Encyclopaedia Britannica, "David Hughes," https://www.britannica.com/biography/David-Hughes (accessed March 13, 2019).
4. Emerson, "The Work of Jagadis Chandra Bose: 100 Years of MM-Wave Research."
5. Emerson, "The Work of Jagadis Chandra Bose: 100 Years of MM-Wave Research."
6. "History of Radar," https://www.blackvalue.de/en/radarbasics/radar-history.html (accessed March 13, 2019).
7. Encyclopaedia Britannica, "Radar," https://www.britannica.com/technology/radar (accessed March 13, 2019).
8. Encyclopaedia Britannica, "Radar."

CHAPTER 4
MICROWAVES AT HOME

1. Evan Ackerman, Institute of Electrical and Electronics Engineers, "A Brief History of the Microwave Oven," https://spectrum.ieee.org/tech-history/space-age/a-brief-history-of-the-microwave-oven (accessed March 13, 2019).

Chapter Notes

2. Timothy J. Jorgensen, "Hot Food, Fast: The Home Microwave Oven Turns 50," Smithsonian.com, https://www.smithsonianmag.com/innovation/hot-food-fast-home-microwave-oven-turns-50-180962545 (accessed March 13, 2019).
3. Jorgensen, "Hot Food, Fast."
4. US Food & Drug Administration, "Microwave Oven Radiation," https://www.fda.gov/radiation-emittingproducts/resourcesforyouradiationemittingproducts/ucm252762.htm (accessed April 8, 2019).
5. Encyclopaedia Britannica, "How Do Microwaves Work?" https://www.britannica.com/story/how-do-microwaves-work (accessed March 13, 2019).
6. The Takeout, "What Does It Mean for Cookware to Be Microwave Safe?" https://thetakeout.com/what-does-it-mean-for-cookware-to-be-microwave-safe-1831162185 (accessed March 13, 2019).
7. George Dvorsky, Io9, "Why Does Your Microwave Oven Mess with the Wi-Fi Connection?" https://io9.gizmodo.com/why-does-your-microwave-oven-mess-with-the-wi-fi-connec-1666117933 (accessed March 13, 2019).
8. John Herman, "Why Everything Wireless Is 2.4 GHz," *Wired*, https://www.wired.com/2010/09/wireless-explainer (accessed March 13, 2019).
9. National Cancer Institute, "Cell Phones and Cancer Risk," https://www.cancer.gov/about-cancer/causes-prevention/risk/radiation/cell-phones-fact-sheet (accessed March 13, 2019).

CHAPTER 5
MICROWAVES AT WORK

1. Michael Shu, "Wireless Power Transmission," http://large.stanford.edu/courses/2011/ph240/shu2 (accessed March 13, 2019).
2. Tracy V. Wilson, HowStuffWorks, "How Wireless Power Works," https://electronics.howstuffworks.com/everyday-tech/wireless-power3.htm (accessed March 13, 2019).
3. U.S. Department of Defense, "Active Denial System FAQs," https://jnlwp.defense.gov/About/Frequently-Asked-Questions/Active-Denial-System-FAQs/ (accessed March 13, 2019).
4. U.S. Department of Defense, Active Denial System FAQs."
5. Encyclopaedia Britannica, "Christian Doppler," https://www.britannica.com/biography/Christian-Doppler (accessed March 13, 2019).
6. National Weather Service, "How Radar Works," https://www.weather.gov/jetstream/how (accessed March 13, 2019).
7. National Weather Service, "How Radar Works."

CHAPTER 6
MICROWAVES IN SPACE

1. NASA Science, "Microwaves," https://science.nasa.gov/ems/06_microwaves (accessed March 13, 2019).
2. NASA, "Tests of Big Bang: The CMB," https://map.gsfc.nasa.gov/universe/bb_tests_cmb.html (accessed March 13, 2019).
3. Encyclopaedia Britannica, "Cosmic Microwave Background," https://www.britannica.com/science/cosmic-microwave-background (accessed March 13, 2019).

Chapter Notes

4. NASA, "Tests of Big Bang: The CMB."
5. Space.com, "Cosmic Microwave Background: Remnant of the Big Bang," https://www.space.com/33892-cosmic-microwave-background.html (accessed March 13, 2019).
6. Space.com, "Cosmic Microwave Background: Remnant of the Big Bang."
7. Encyclopaedia Britannica, "Satellite Communication," https://www.britannica.com/technology/satellite-communication (accessed March 13, 2019).
8. Encyclopaedia Britannica, "Satellite Communication."
9. "How Does GPS Work?" http://www.physics.org/article-questions.asp?id=55 (accessed March 13, 2019).
10. "How Does GPS Work?"
11. European Space Agency, "How Satellite Navigation Works," http://m.esa.int/Our_Activities/Navigation/How_satellite_navigation_works (accessed March 13, 2019).

GLOSSARY

COSMIC MICROWAVE BACKGROUND Electromagnetic radiation that is left over from the Big Bang and fills the universe.

DOPPLER EFFECT The change in frequency relative to motion.

KLYSTRON A type of electron tube that creates or amplifies microwaves by controlling the speed of a stream of electrons.

MAGNETRON A type of vacuum tube that creates an electric field.

MASER A type of device that creates and amplifies microwaves.

MECHANICAL WAVE A wave that requires a medium, such as ocean waves that travel in the medium of water.

OSCILLATOR A device that produces alternating electric current.

PARTICLE ACCELERATOR A device that produces a beam of fast-moving charged particles.

PLASMA A collection of electrically charged particles.

RADIATION Energy emitted in the form of waves or particles.

SEMICONDUCTOR A substance whose conductivity is between that of a conductor and an insulator.

TRANSISTOR A device that controls the flow of electricity in electronic equipment.

FURTHER READING

BOOKS

Bright, Michael. *The Big Bang and Beyond*. New York, NY: PowerKids Press, 2018.

Reed, Cristie. *Microwave Ovens*. Vero Beach, FL: Rourke Educational Media, 2015.

Resler, Tamara J. *How Things Work: Discover Secrets and Science Behind Bounce Houses, Hovercraft, Robotics, and Everything in Between*. Washington, DC: National Geographic, 2016.

Sears, Kathleen. *Weather 101*. New York, NY: Adams Media, 2017.

WEBSITES

HowStuffWorks: How Microwave Cooking Works
https://home.howstuffworks.com/microwave.htm
Find out how microwave ovens cook food.

Planck Mission
http://planck.cf.ac.uk
Learn more about the Planck Mission, a satellite that measured the cosmic microwave background, and what it found.

Tour of the Electromagnetic Spectrum: Microwaves
https://science.nasa.gov/ems/06_microwaves
NASA describes where microwaves come from and how they are detected.

INDEX

A

absorption 10, 12, 14, 29, 31–33
Active Denial System 40–41
Alpher, Ralph 45–46
altimeter 51–52
atmosphere 10, 11–12, 26, 44, 51
atoms 10, 13–14, 18, 30, 46

B

background radiation 48
ball lightning 14
bands 8–12, 35
Big Bang 15–16, 45–48
blueshift 15
Bose, Jagadish Chandra 23–24

C

cell phones 34, 35
CMB radiation 13, 15–16, 45–48
communications technology 4, 10, 12, 18, 20, 21, 24, 27, 28, 34–35, 49
curing 38

D

dark matter 48
Dicke, Robert 45–46
Doppler, Christian 42
Doppler effect 41, 42–44
drying 38

E

electromagnetic field 4, 5, 16–17, 19–20,
electromagnetic spectrum 6, 8, 10, 15, 35
energy transmission 38–40

F

Faraday, Michael 21–22
frequency 6, 8–12, 15, 17, 18, 19–20, 25, 26, 34–35, 41, 42–43, 48

G

gamma rays 8, 14, 15, 48
GPS 11, 49–51

H

Hertz, Heinrich 22–23, 25
Hughes, David 23

Index

Hülsmeyer Christian, 25

I

ionizing radiation 30

J

Jupiter 15

K

klystron 19–20

L

laser 17–18
lidar 25
lightning 14–16, 33

M

magnetron 13, 19–20, 26, 28–29, 30
Marconi, Guglielmo 24
maser 17–18
Maxwell, James Clerk 21–22
mechanical waves 4, 43
microwave ovens 6, 13, 20, 21, 28–33, 35, 36
military 25–26, 40–41, 49

N

National Weather Service 44

non-ionizing radiation 30, 35
nuclear technology 48

O

opaque 10, 25, 46
oscillator 16

P

particle accelerators 20
Penzias, Arno 45–46, 48
photons 6, 14, 16, 18, 46
plasma 14, 46

R

radar 20, 24–26, 29, 41–44, 51–52
radar gun 41
radiant heating 29
radio devices 4, 12, 16, 19, 24, 45, 49
radiometer 51
radio waves 7–8, 10, 13–14, 15, 26, 30, 35, 41
rainbow 4
rectifier 38–40
redshift 15, 48
reflection 23, 25, 31, 33, 52
refraction 23
remote sensing 51–53

63

S

safety 30–33, 35
satellites 12, 40, 49–53
semiconductor 16
solid-state devices 16–18, 23
speed of light 5, 22, 51
Spencer, Percy L. 28–29
stars 13, 48
surface heating 36–37

T

telescopes 18
television 19, 20, 34, 35, 48, 49
transistor 16, 18, 19, 27
transparent 10–11, 25

V

vacuum-tube devices 13, 16, 18–20
visible light 4, 5, 6, 8, 13, 14, 15, 17–18, 22–23, 25
volumetric heating 37–38

W

wavelength 4–6, 7–10, 24, 26, 44
weather forecasting 36, 42, 44, 52–53
Wi-Fi 12, 34–35
Wilson, Robert 45–46, 48
wind scatterometer 52–53
World War II 21, 25–26, 28, 42

X

X-ray 4, 8, 14, 48